DAT CARVING ESSENTIALS

DAT Carving Essentials:

Soap Carving for the Canadian Dental Aptitude Test (DAT)

Oscar Willis

Copyright © 2020 by Oscar Willis

All rights reserved.

No part of this book may be reproduced in any form or by any electronic or mechanical means including information storage and retrieval systems, without permission in writing from the author. The only exception is by a reviewer, who may quote short excerpts in a review.

Printed in Canada

Table of Contents

Introduction 1

Carving Section of the DAT 2

Materials 3

Examining the Drawing 4

Marking 6

    The Triangle 6

    The Box 12

    The Diamond 18

    Variation of the basic end shape patterns 25

    3D Diagrams of End Shapes or Patterns 31

    Summary diagram of the different variations of end shapes 32

    Longitudinal and Circumferential Marking Lines 32

    Cut Surfaces 34

Time Allocation for Carving 35

Knife holding technique 36

Types of Carving 36

    Bulk Carving 36

    Fine Carving 36

    Polishing Techniques 37

Carving Components of the Soap 37

    Carving Notches..37

    Carving Flutes..38

    Carving Saddles...38

Final Product...38

Warnings...39

Exam Day..39

Practice Problems...41

Introduction

The Canadian DAT manual dexterity component is unique compared to the American DAT and other professional graduate entrance exams. The Canadian DAT is acceptable in Canada and the United States but not vice versa. Therefore, there is motivation for writing a single exam that is accepted in North America. The carving section of the Canadian DAT requires a certain amount of manual dexterity that can be developed through practice. The appropriate knowledge facilitates rapid improvement in carving skills and may lead to dramatic improve carving scores. Knowledge and experience will lead to quicker improvements minimize unnecessary trial and error. Review the information in this book as many times as necessary to master soap carving. Soap carving diagrams allow you to practice, apply knowledge, and develop soap carving skills. The manual dexterity section of the DAT can be taught, trained and developed through knowledge and practice.

Carving Section of the DAT

The Dental Aptitude Test (DAT) is a required test for admission into a Canadian or American dental school. The Canadian DAT is different from the American DAT by having a carving section. The carving section requires the applicant to carve a cylindrically shaped soap according to the shape and dimensions given in the exam. The carving section is the first component of the DAT. The applicant is given 30 minutes to carve the soap. The other sections of the DAT include, in order, the natural sciences section which includes 40 questions for biology and 30 questions for chemistry in 60 minutes. The American DAT includes organic chemistry in the chemistry section while the Canadian DAT does not. The natural science section is followed by the perceptual ability section which includes 6 sections with 15 questions per section for 60 minutes. The last component of the DAT is the English comprehension section and includes 3 passages with 15-17 questions per passage with 50 minutes of time allotted. Most of the DAT requires academic studying that is not foreign to most students applying. However, the carving section of the DAT is a manual dexterity test that is unique to the DAT compared to other professional school admission tests. Fortunately, the DAT carving section involves a level of carving that can be developed with practice and the correct knowledge of planning, approach, and understanding of the test. Knowledge, proper planning, and approach to the carving section are one of the most important keys to scoring high. It constitutes the bulk of the requirements to successfully complete the section. This information will be covered, and you will be well on your way in your journey to a high scoring carving section. Practice to develop proper technique and control is important and will be explained in later sections along with practice activities. Practice problems will be available in the end to let you put together the strategic plan, knowledge, and carving in a problem like the actual soap carving exam.

Materials

The carving material is standardized and provided by the Canadian Dental Association. The material can be purchased from CDA online (http://www.cda-adc.ca/) . The dental preparation kit is a package by the CDA that includes a knife handle, knife blade, six pieces of soap, a Sharpie marker, flexible ruler, and a booklet describing the test. Extra soaps can be bought in packages of 6 pieces for extra practice. Most applicants purchase an additional 2 or 3 soap packages. In general, many applicants are proficient after carving approximately 18 pieces of soap. The knife blade often dulls after carving approximately 12 pieces of soap. The knife blade can be sharpened, or additional blades are available for purchase from the CDA website. Many applicants remove the backing of the flexible ruler to facilitate marking of the soap. Many applicants use the pencil instead of the marker to mark the soap. The marker often becomes clogged by the soap to be unusable. In addition to the materials provided by the kit, you will want to add a pair of latex gloves, bandages, several sharpened pencils with round shafts instead of beveled shafts, and a pencil sharpener. The latex gloves are useful because it will keep you from getting perspiration on the soap, especially under the stress of the real exam. The perspiration will cause the soap shavings to stick to the cylinder in clumps to ruin your carving, cover the markings, make the soap slippery and make carving very difficult. The size of the latex gloves should be the right fit or even a size smaller to give you more sensitivity. Latex gloves are preferable to nitrile gloves because of added sensitivity. Nitrile gloves are acceptable if people are allergic to latex. Several bandages should be available to you when you carve in case you or someone else gets cut while carving. In general, there is usually at least one person who cuts themselves during the DAT. Additional pencils should be brought with you to the exam in case the pencil chips or breaks. You don't want to waste time sharpening or be without a pencil during the exam. A pencil sharpener is needed in case all your pencils break. The recommended number of pencils you should bring is about five pencils. There have been cases where all five pencils break and the person was forced to use a pencil sharpener. Pencils should have a round shaft instead of the beveled shafts provided on the exam. The round pencil shaft ensures smooth and uniform markings for longitudinal lines that will be described later. Mechanical pencils are not advised because the tip of the pencil will be different each time the lead is broken.

Examining the Drawing

You have 5 minutes to examine the drawing provided for you to carve. During these 5 minutes you have the opportunity to understand the diagram and work-out a plan on the paper provided. You are not allowed to make any markings on the soap. You will be provided with six views of the drawing you are to carve. The views include the side view, top view, bottom view, two end views, and two 3D views. When examining the drawings, you should note the dimensions and components you need to carve. Every soap drawing will require you to carve three components including the left end, right end, and middle. The dimensions of the soap are 84 mm for the shaft and 16 mm for the diameter. You should memorize the dimensions because it will be useful when measuring and calculating carving dimensions from the drawing. An example of a typical carving drawing that you would encounter on a DAT exam is shown on the next page to allow you to be familiar with the layout of a carving problem.

All measurements are in millimetres
(not necessarily drawn to scale)

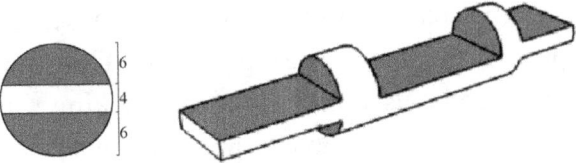

Directions for Carving:

The illustrations near the top show how the carving should appear when it is completed.

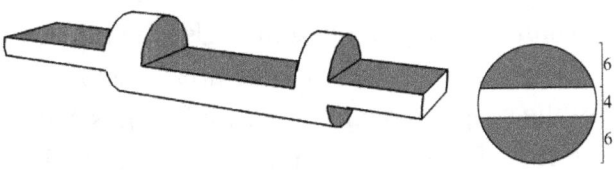

The carving exercise consists of 3 parts (2 end and 1 surface pattern). It is important that all 3 parts be completed to be considered for high scoring.

You may use the small ridge on the top and bottom as midlines for carving relationships.

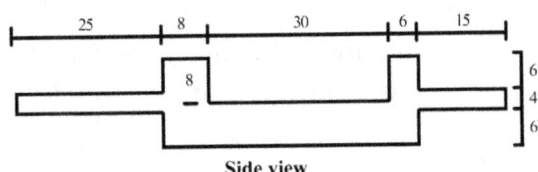

Side view

The dimensions should be followed as closely as possible. The carving will be evaluated on accurate and complete reproduction of the pattern in measurements and design, smoothness and flatness of planes, sharpness of angles, symmetry and orientation of the 3 parts.

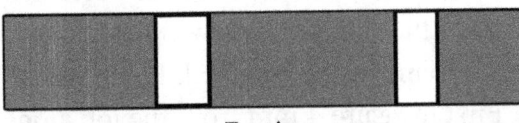

Top view

DIRECTIONS FOR HANDING IN THE CARVING:

1. Print your name, identification number and test centre code on an uncut surface of your carving and also on the napkin.

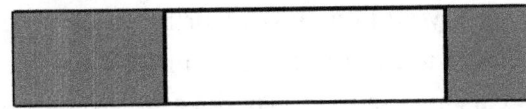

Bottom view

2. Wrap your carving carefully and securely so that it may be shipped safely for grading. Fold the napkin in such a way that the carving will not fall out.

Shaded area denotes cut surface.
*This dimension can vary depending on the overall length of the carving.

3. Hand in your wrapped carving to your evaluation proctor.

Marking

After you examine the drawing and before you carve, you need to mark the soap to define the areas you will carve. First mark the ends because it will provide the basis for the other markings along the shaft. When facing the end of the soap, you will notice a line along the middle generated as part of the manufacturing process. This line will always be in the middle and can be used for part of the marking. Conventionally, the original line down the middle is oriented so that it is vertical. The subsequent diagrams will represent this line with a dashed line. Another reference point you will want to mark is the midpoint along this manufacturer generated line. Use the ruler provided to mark this midpoint along the manufacturer generated line. We know the diameter of the soap is 14 mm so the midpoint is found by measuring 7 mm from either side along the original line. A tick mark using the pencil can be used to mark this reference midpoint. From now on it is recommended to measure from the center tick instead of from the edge for more accuracy. There are three different types of ends that you should recognize. Any shape that you may encounter will be a variation of these three shapes.

The Triangle

The first end shape is the triangle. The method will be described in brief along with pointers and then explained step by step. To measure and mark the triangle, you will need to know and remember that each side of the triangle will be equal. Each side of the triangle will measure 14 mm. First measure 4 mm from the top along the center line from the edge. Alternatively, measure 3 mm up from the midpoint and place a tick mark with your pencil. Measuring from the midpoint instead of the edge is more accurate. In the exam you will be given the 4 mm dimension in the carving diagram. That is all the measurements you need to make for marking the triangle. The marking of the triangle will be explained step by step with diagrams on the next page. We will now briefly explain it to give you a general idea. Draw a horizontal line at the 4 mm mark that spans from edge to edge. The horizontal line will be the top side of the triangle. Then draw a line joining the left end of the horizontal line with bottom end of the center line to construct the left side of the triangle. Finally, draw a line from the right end of the horizontal line to the bottom of the center line to construct the right side of the triangle. There are a couple of methods to mark these straight lines. The first method is to use a pencil and ruler to mark the lines. The second method is to use the blade of the knife to gently press on the soap to draw straight lines. Using the blade to mark straight lines is recommended because it is quicker and is guaranteed to be always straight.

Next, the marking of the triangle will be explained step-by-step with diagrams.

Step 1: Mark the middle of the center line with a tick mark.

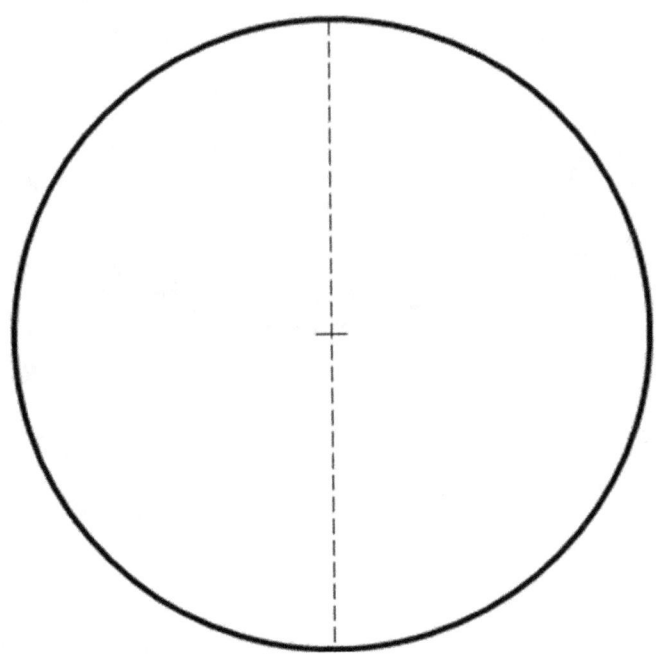

Step 2: Measure 4 mm from the top along the center line either from the edge or measure 3 mm up from the midpoint. Place a tick mark with your pencil.

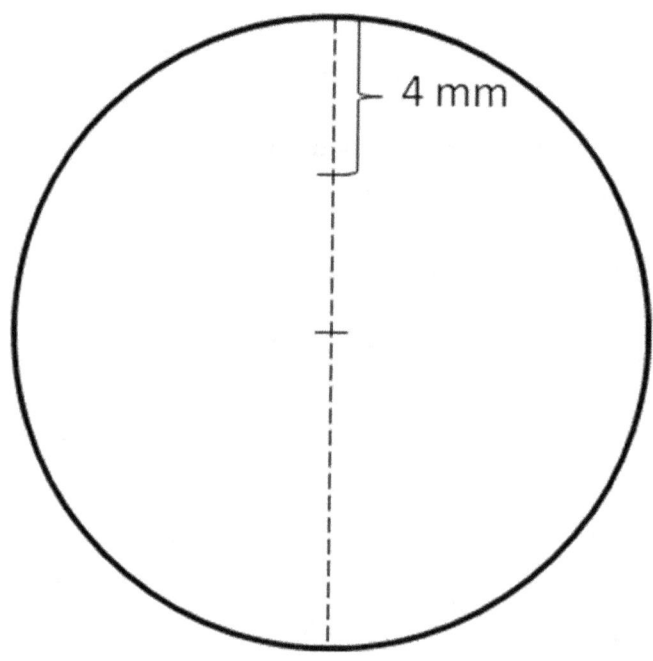

8

Step 3: Draw a horizontal line at the 4 mm mark all the way across the soap.

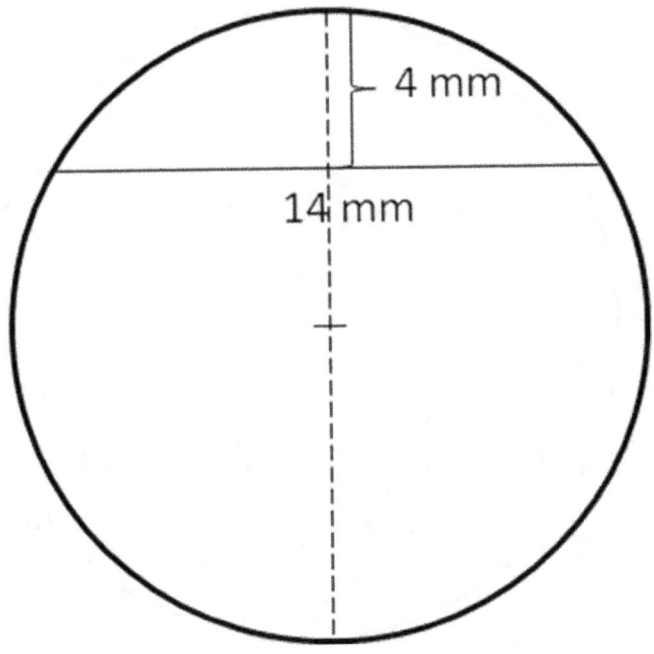

Step 4: Draw a line joining the left end of the horizontal line with bottom end of the center line to construct the left side of the triangle.

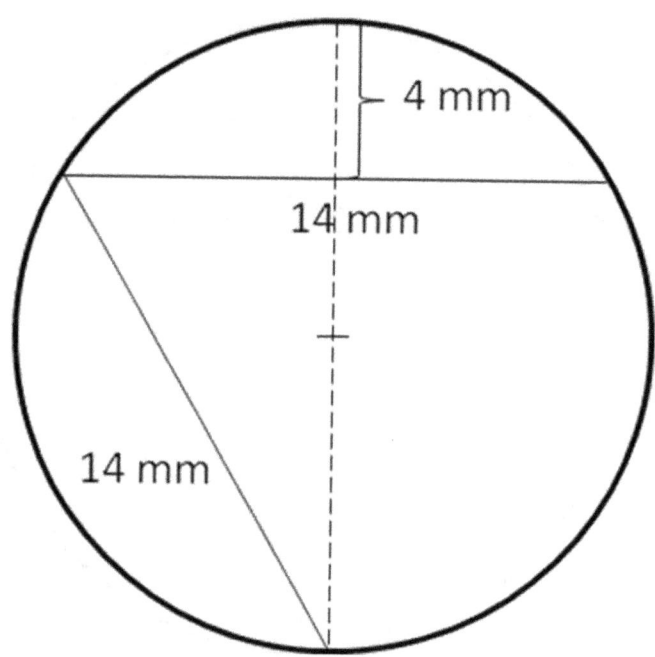

10

Step 5: Draw a line from the right end of the horizontal line to the bottom of the center line to construct the right side of the triangle.

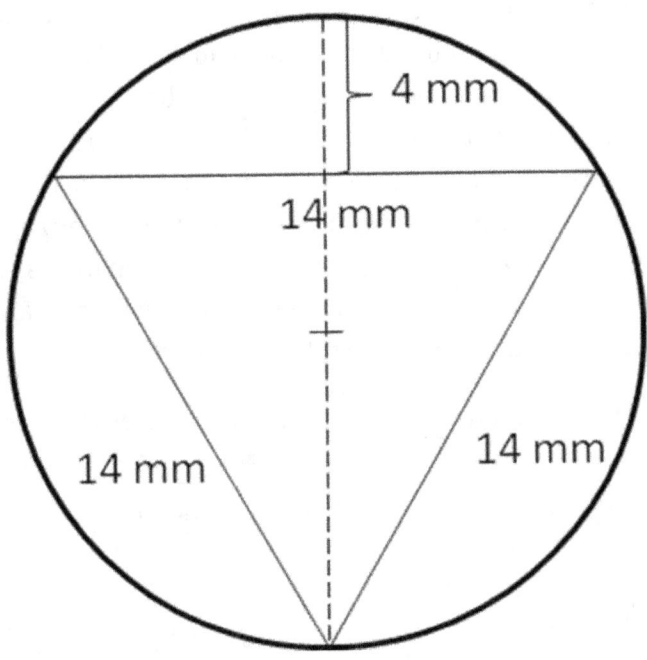

The Box

A brief description of marking the box end shape will be followed by step by step explanations. A slight variation is introduced in the step-by-step explanations. Slight variations are introduced to suit the personal preference of the carver.

The box begins by finding the midpoint and marking a tick. Each side of the box will be 11 mm, and half way of 11 mm is 5.5 mm. Measure 5.5 mm from the midpoint on the right side and mark it with a tick. Repeat and measure 5.5 mm on the left side of the midpoint and make a tick mark. Then mark a straight vertical line using the blade or pencil with ruler at one of the tick marks until you reach the edges of the soap. Repeat marking a vertical line on the tick mark on the other side so that you have a vertical line that reaches the edges of the soap at the position of the tick mark. The next step is to mark a straight horizontal line between the top ends of both vertical lines. Then mark a straight horizontal line between the bottom ends of the two vertical lines. The result is a square marked on the end of the soap.

Next, we will explain how to mark the box end step-by-step with diagrams.

Step 1: Mark the middle of the center line with a tick mark.

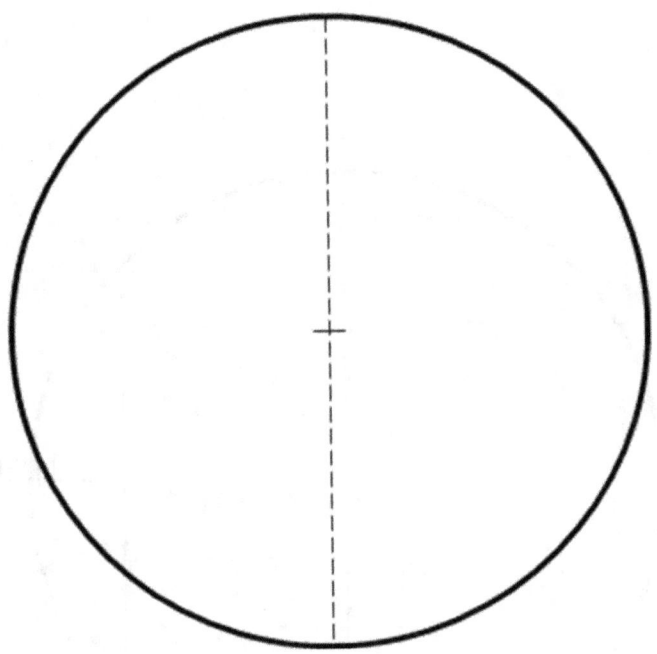

Step 2: Measure 5.5 mm from the midpoint on the right side and mark with a tick. Mark a straight vertical line using the blade or pencil with ruler at one of the tick marks until you reach the edges of the soap.

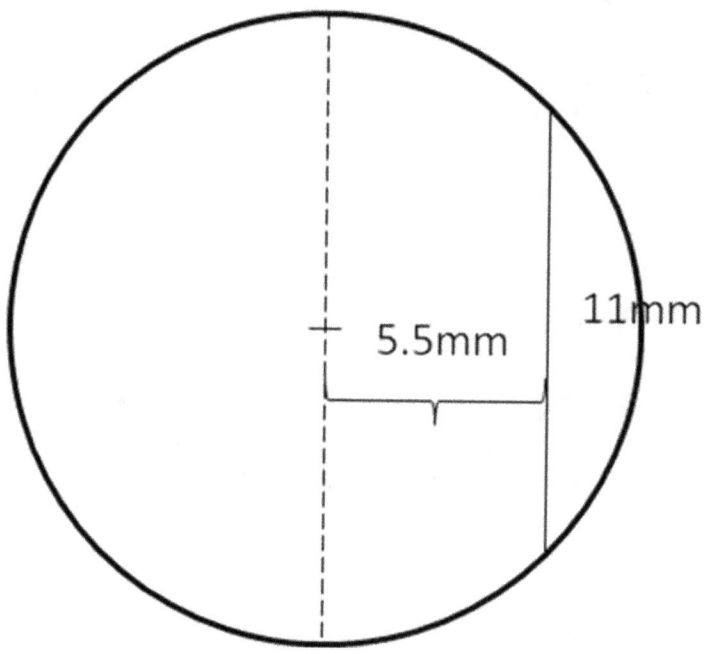

Step 3: Measure 5.5 mm on the left side of the midpoint and make a tick mark. Mark a straight vertical line using the blade or pencil with ruler at one of the tick marks until you reach the edges of the soap.

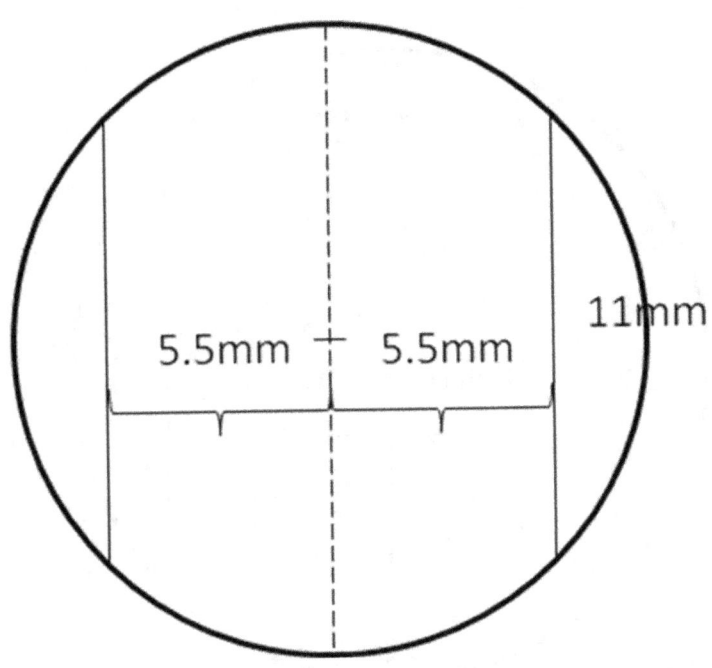

Step 4: Mark a straight horizontal line between the top ends of both vertical lines.

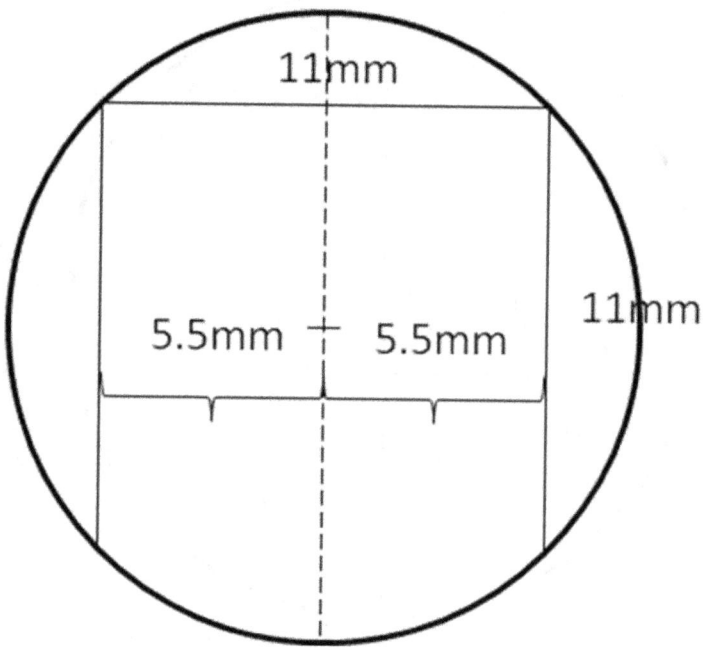

Step 5: Mark a straight horizontal line between the bottom ends of the two vertical lines.

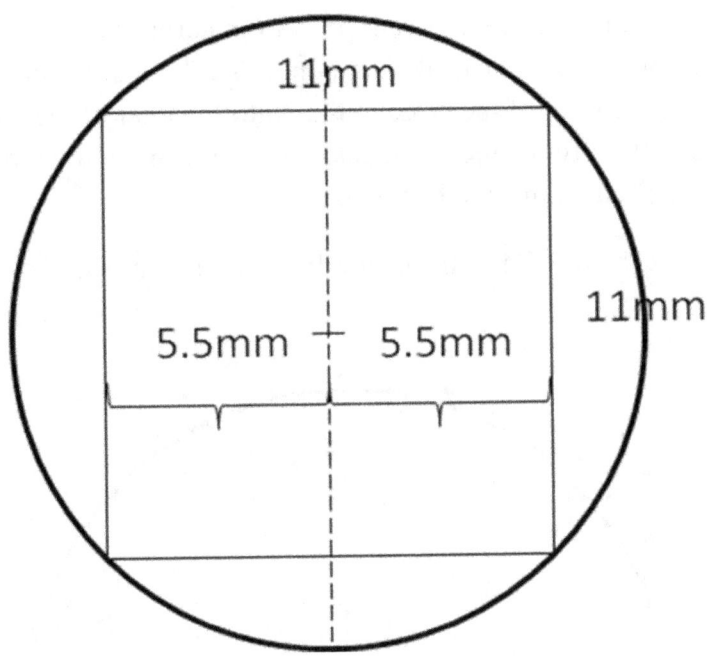

The Diamond

The last end shape is the diamond. The diamond begins by finding the midpoint of the center line. Then mark a horizontal straight line at the midpoint tick so that the horizontal line extends to the ends of the soap. You should see a cross marked on the end of the soap. Next mark a straight line from the top corner of the cross to the left corner of the cross to create the upper left side of the diamond. Then mark a straight line from the top corner of the cross to the right corner of the cross to create the upper right side of the diamond. Then mark a straight line from the left corner of the cross to the bottom corner of the cross to create the bottom left side of the diamond. Finally, mark a straight line from the right corner of the cross to the bottom corner of the cross to create the bottom right side of the diamond. You should be looking at a diamond marked on the end of the soap.

Step 1: Mark the middle of the center line with a tick mark.

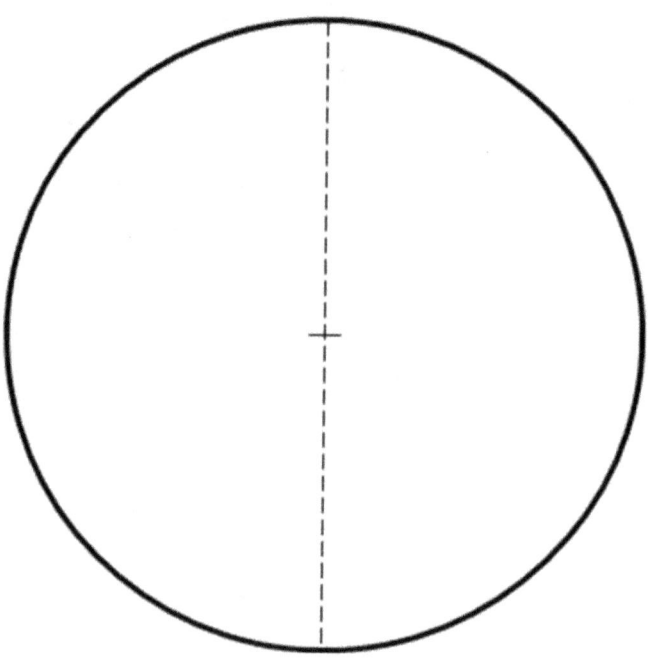

Step 2: Mark a horizontal straight line at the midpoint tick so that the horizontal line extends to the ends of the soap.

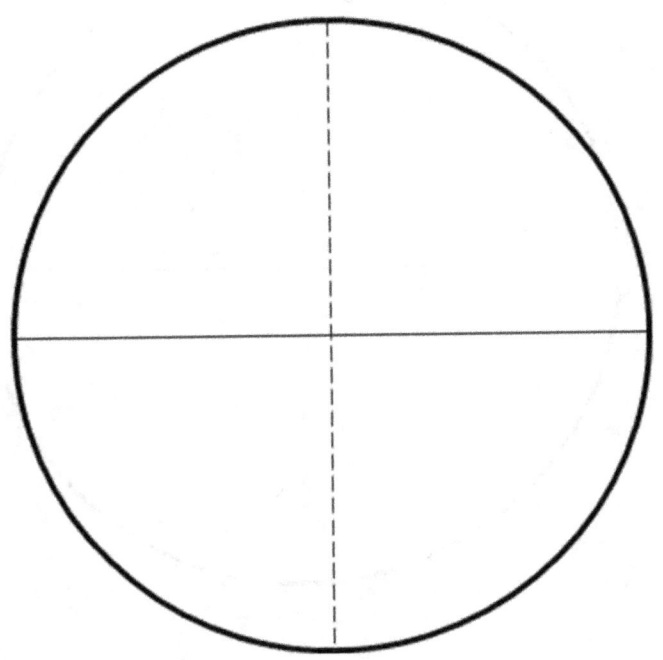

Step 3: Mark a straight line from the top corner of the cross to the left corner of the cross to create the upper left side of the diamond.

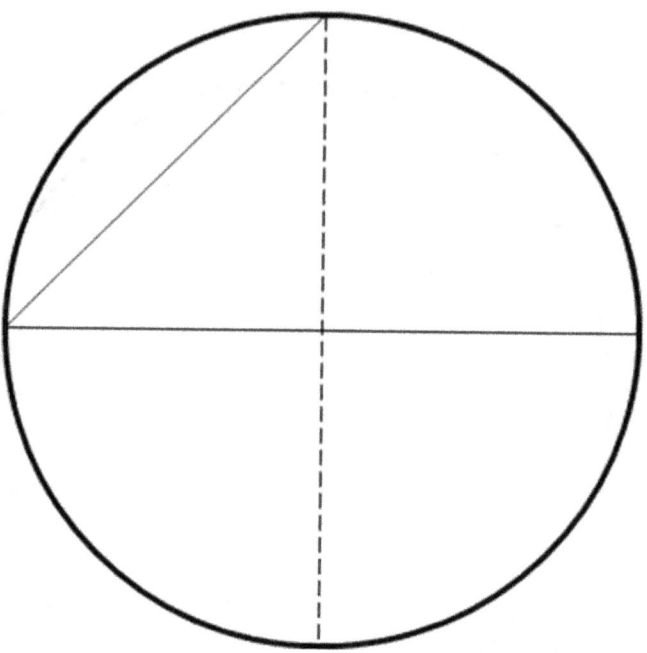

Step 4: Mark a straight line from the top corner of the cross to the right corner of the cross to create the upper right side of the diamond.

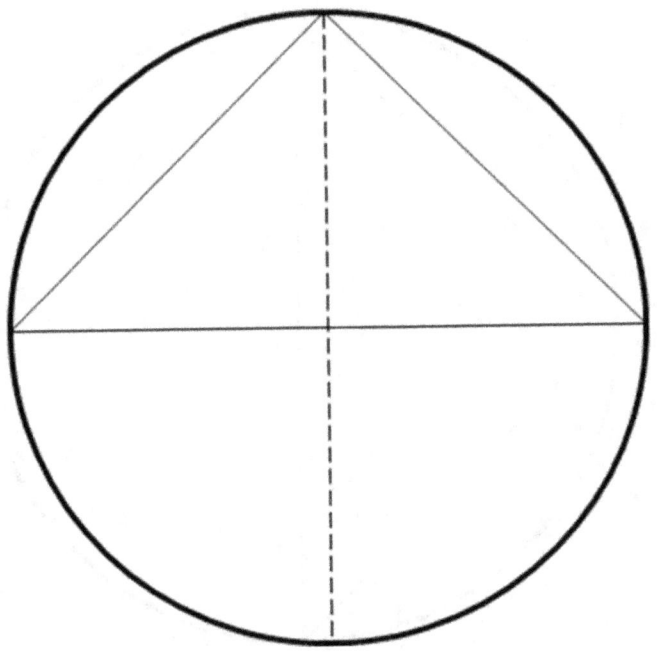

Step 5: Mark a straight line from the left corner of the cross to the bottom corner of the cross to create the bottom left side of the diamond.

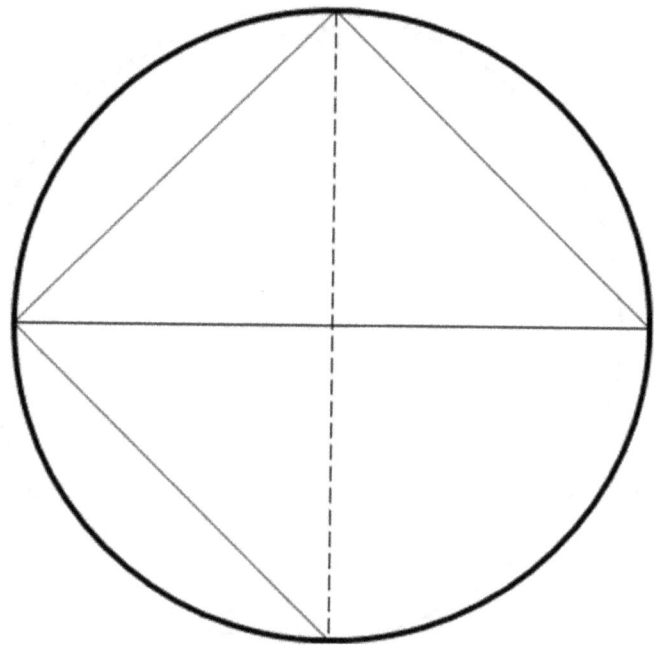

Step 6: Mark a straight line from the right corner of the cross to the bottom corner of the cross to create the bottom right side of the diamond.

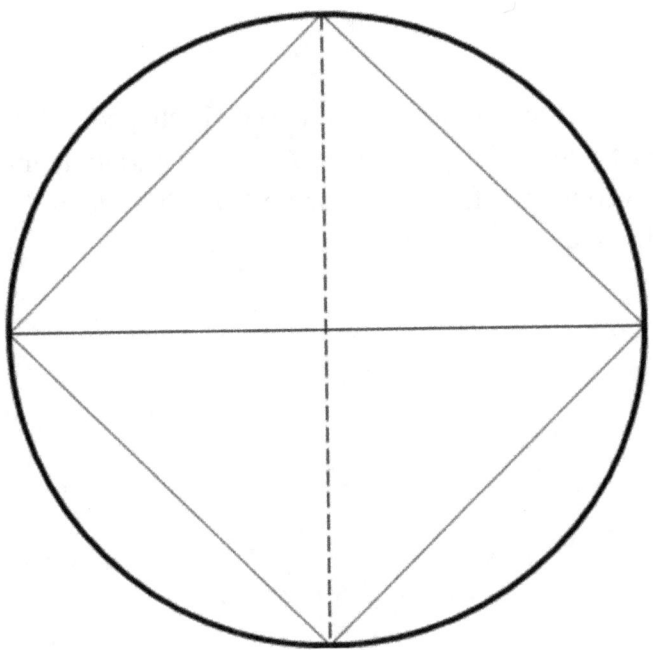

The other variations of the triangle, box, and diamond can be generated by two factors. The first factor is simply marking a smaller size of these shapes and the second factor is the choice of two cut surfaces known as the notch or flute. The smaller shape of the triangle, box and diamond are shown below. The two types of cut surfaces are shown. The notch is simply a cut perpendicularly into end of the soap meeting with a cut perpendicular to the shaft of the soap. A flute is like the notch but instead of perpendicular sides, the flute has a slope that extends from a point on the shaft to a place on end of the soap.

There are two other variations of the triangle shaped end. One variation is cutting perpendicularly along the sides of the triangle into the soap. The other variation is to cut at an angle from the side of the triangle into the soap to give you a slanted bevel.

Variation of the basic end shape patterns

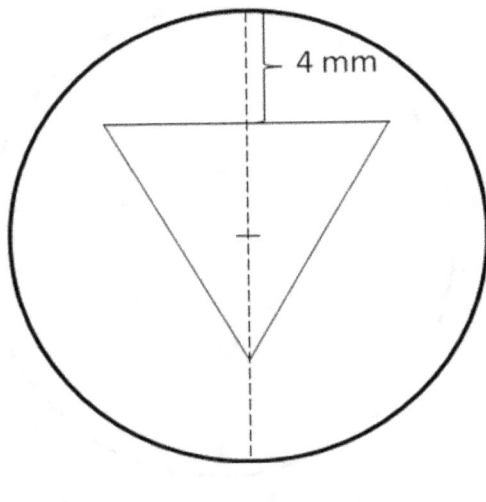

End View

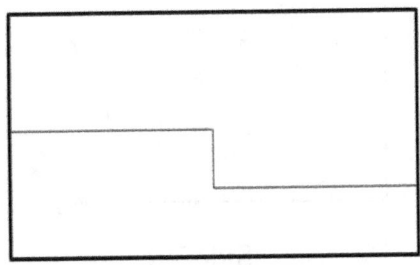

Side View

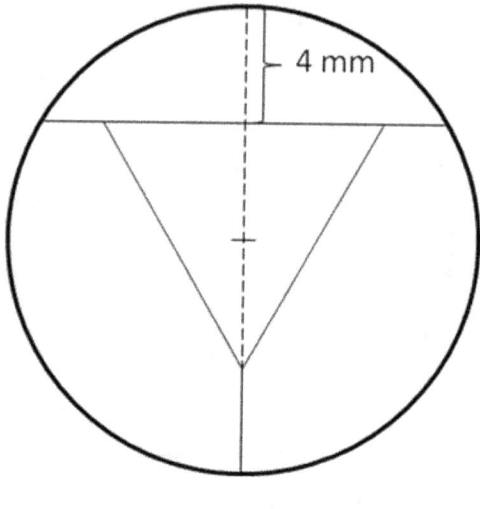

End View

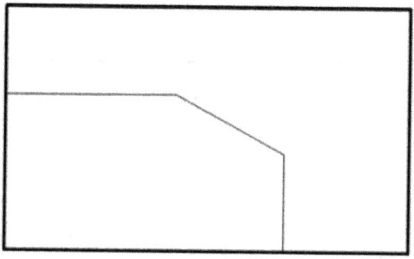

Side View

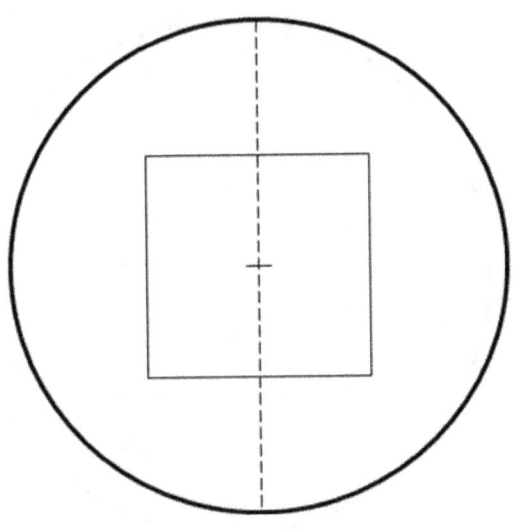

End View

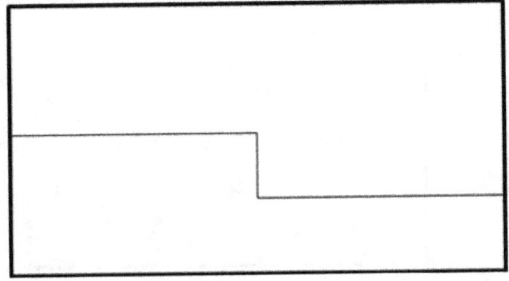

Side View

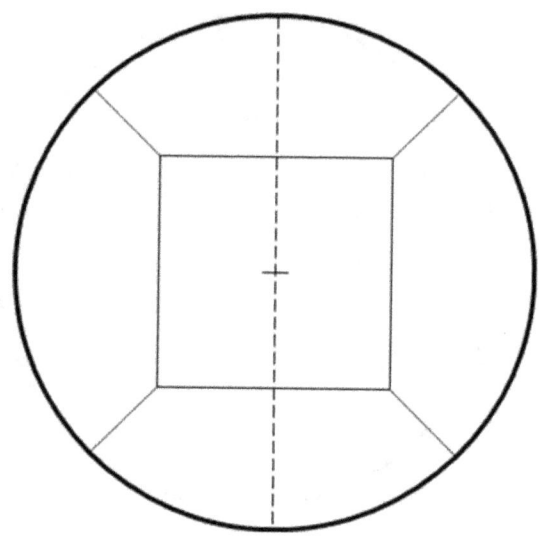

End View

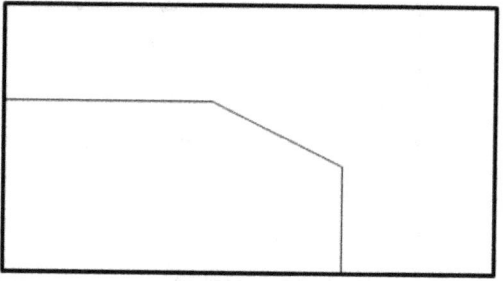

Side View

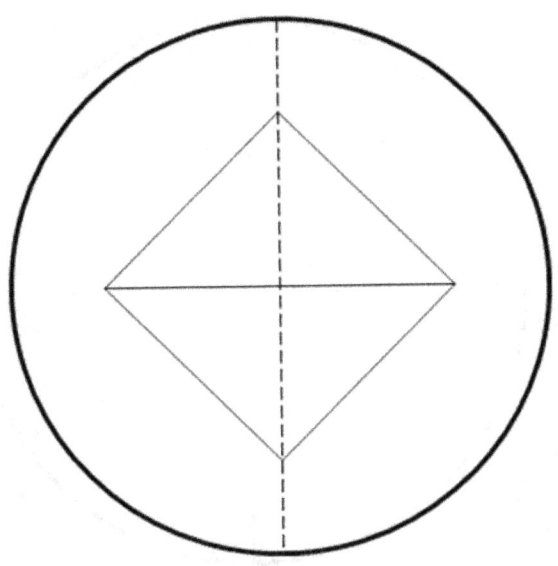

End View

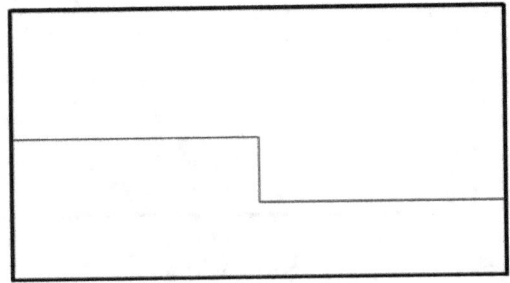

Side View

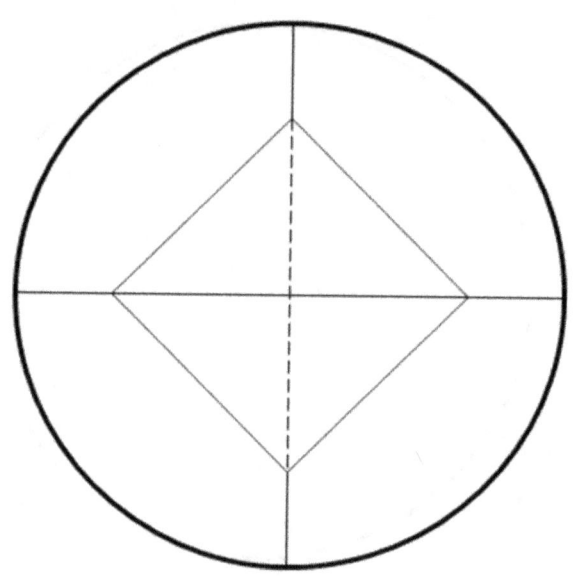

End View

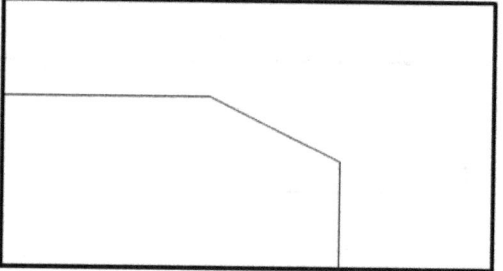

Side View

3D Diagrams of End Shapes or Patterns

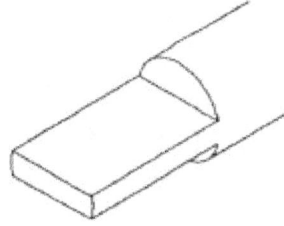 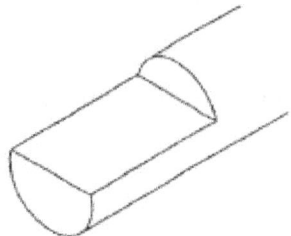

Single or double notched ends

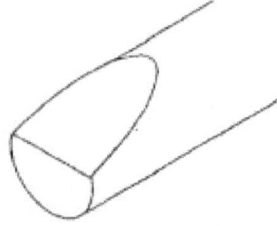 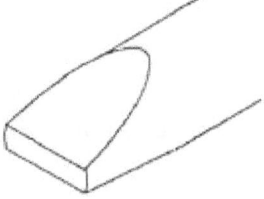

Single or double fluted ends

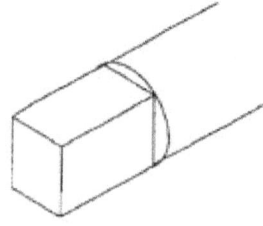 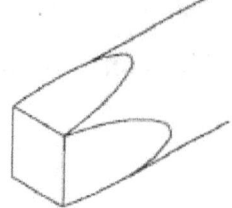

Square end (fluted or notched)

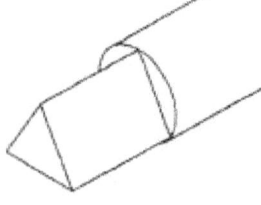 

Triangle end (fluted or notched)

Summary diagram of the different variations of end shapes.

Summary of diagram of the various different end shapes are shown on the next page.

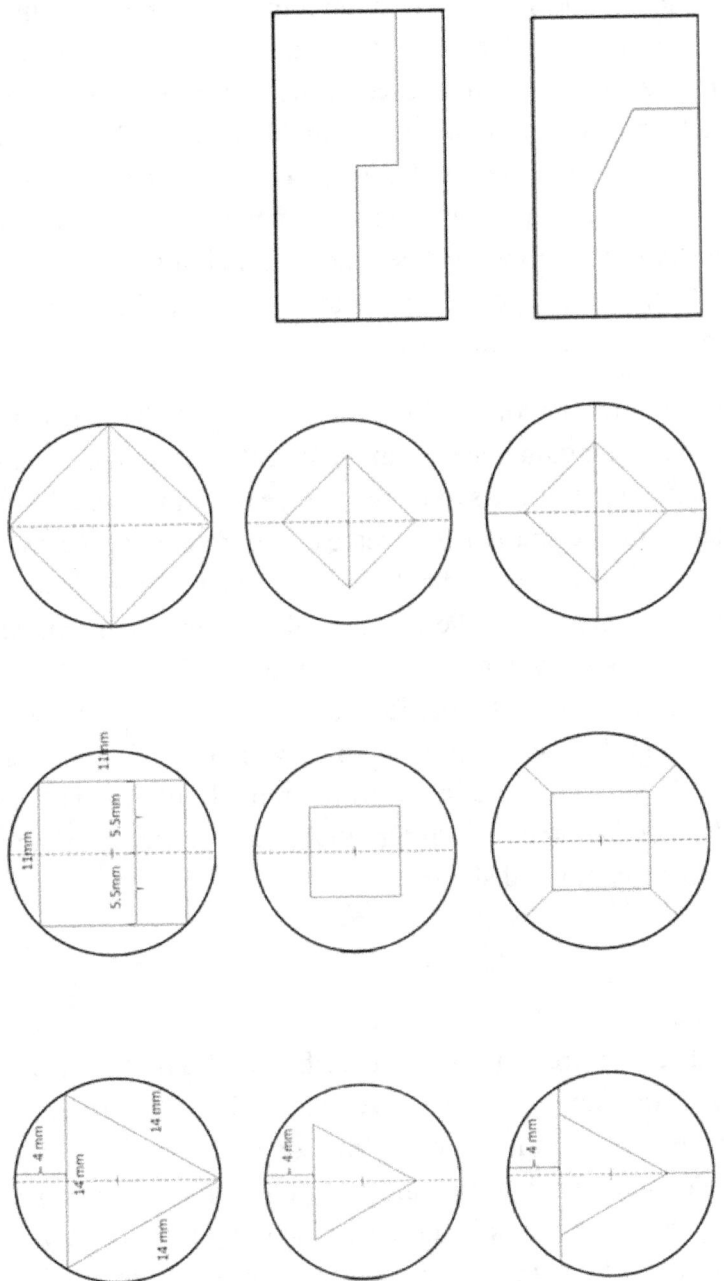

Longitudinal and Circumferential Marking Lines

Once you have the ends of the soap marked, you are ready to create lines along the shaft of the soap. Longitudinal lines are lines that run parallel to the shaft of the soap. You want to create longitudinal lines that run the length of the soap and begin at each of the corner of the triangle, box, or diamond. To create a straight longitudinal line, place the soap on a flat surface or table. Align the tip of the pencil with the corner of the end shape and have the pencil flat against the table. Then glide the pencil along the shaft the soap while keeping the pencil always in contact with the table. You would repeat the process to draw longitudinal lines for each of the corner of the end shape.

The next step after the longitudinal lines is to mark the dimension of the saddle or the rectangular carving in the middle of the soap. Measure and mark the dimension of the saddle by using a ruler and pencil to create tick marks along the shaft. Then create circumferential lines that wrap around the shaft to mark the depth of the saddle to carve. To create circumferential lines, wrap the flexible ruler around the soap. Align the ruler with the tick mark you made for the saddle. Then use the pencil to follow along the edge of the flexible ruler to draw a line that wraps around the soap. Repeat the process to draw another circumferential lines. Usually you will need two circumferential lines to mark the saddle depth. Also need another circumferential line for each end shape to mark the depth to carve for end shapes.

Cut Surfaces

There are three different types of cut surfaces. The first is the notch and the second is the flute which we covered. The last cut surface is the saddle or the cutout in the middle of the soap. The saddle is made from two perpendicular cuts into the middle of the shaft of the soap and a cut connecting the two perpendicular cuts. The saddle varies only in dimensions and will always be present in a carving problem. When carving at home, you will gain a lot of practice with carving saddles and will be able to carve the saddle fairly quickly.

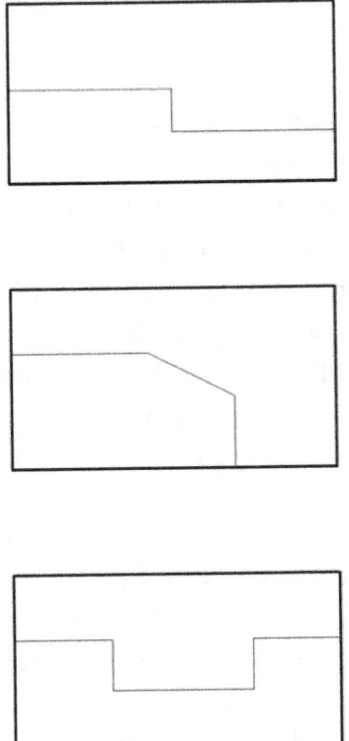

Time Allocation for Carving

You will be given 5 minutes to examine the soap to ensure the soap is free from chips or deformities. Then another 5 minutes is provided to examine the drawing when you can plan out how you will carve the diagram. During this time, you can draw on the diagram but not on the soap. Then you will be given 30 minutes to carve. You want to spend 5 minutes but preferably 4 minutes to mark the soap. This is a critical stage that you want to practice to do quickly. You can save a lot of time on this stage in marking the soap. Remember that the marking is also critical to an accurate carving so quality cannot be sacrificed for speed. Then you can spend 10 minutes on bulk carving to give the general shape of the carving. The next 10 minutes is to refine the carving. The last 5 minutes to polish the carving and double check your work.

Knife holding technique

The blade of the knife can be removed by loosening the nut in the knife handle. Then place the knife in a direction that is comfortable. In general, the knife blade should be switched such that the flat part of the handle rests in your palm and the blade is facing you. Hold the handle of the blade such that the blade is perpendicular to your forearm. Most of the carving will be done by pulling the blade towards you. Place the thumb on the soap as leverage when you pull the blade towards you. For more control and force, have your hands hold closer to the blade.

Types of Carving

The main types of carving are bulk carving, fine carving, and polishing. The bulk carving is done at the beginning to give the general shape of the soap carving. The fine carving follows bulk carving and is supposed to bring the carving close to the final product. Finally, the polishing is done to make the final carving very smooth and have crisp edges.

Bulk Carving

Bulk carving is rapidly shaving off as much of the soap as you can without digging so deep as to make the soap crumble or chip. You want to create the shape you want to carve but leave a few millimeters of soap from the marking lines. You will carve every component of the soap beginning with the ends and ending with the saddle.

Fine Carving

Now that you are close to the marking lines, you will have to be very careful not to carve too much or to ruin the shape. So, you will continue to carve but shave off very thin pieces each time. When you get proficient, you can still perform this stage very quickly by carving more rapidly and not carving more deeply.

Polishing Techniques

Once you have reached the shape you want, you can perform a few polishing techniques to really bring the soap carving to the next level and it will only take a few minutes. If there are any small inconsistencies or uneven planes, you can remove very small amounts of soap. You can hold the handle such that the blade faces towards you or away from you. The grip doesn't need to be tight because you want to move the blade very lightly over the soaps surface and remove so little soap that you see light fluffy almost snow-like shavings. You may want to practice this technique on old soap to become very good at this technique because it is very useful in performing emergency recovery of uneven surfaces. The next polishing technique is used to create a matte and flat surface instead of a shiny surface. This technique involves placing the blade over the soap and brushing the blade across the surface to remove a peel of soap. Care and practice are required because you are placing the sharp side of the knife blade on the surface of your almost finished carving and you don't want to create knife marks on the surface. But when you master this polishing technique you will be able to create a very clean matte-like effect and even use this technique to flatten out surface or remove bumps or marks on the surface.

Carving Components of the Soap

Carving Notches

Notches are carved by first sliding the knife blade a few millimeters from the border of the marking line you created earlier to create a safety marking. Then slowly carve from the edge at the end of the soap towards the safety marking. After you have carved about half the depth of the notch you will need to start carving and defining the wall of the notch by cutting vertically slivers at a time. As you progress closer to the border you will need to alternate from the wall and the floor of the notch in order to keep the corners sharp and to prevent uneven planes.

Carving Flutes

Begin by marking the upper boundary of the flute by scoring the soap a few millimeters from the boundary. Then scrape soap away from you starting from the end way from the end of the soap. You want to create a gradual tapering effect and there is no defined angle for the slope. One of the most common problems with flutes is that the flute will scoop or instead of a flat sloping plane you will get a concave curve for the flute. A way to prevent scooping of the flute is the also carve with the blade being pulled towards you while the end the slope is facing you. You want to carve towards you and alternate carving to the left and right.

Carving Saddles

Saddles can be carved by creating vertical lines close to the boundary by a few millimeters to create safety lines. Then dig the knife to create a "V" in the middle of the saddle followed by cutting vertically to flatten the sides of the saddle. Then use the blade to carve horizontally to flatten the base of the saddle. These initial aggressive cuts are to quickly arrive at the shape of the saddle. Then you will alternate carving downwards on the sides and flatten the base of the saddle to progressively reach the boundaries of the saddle.

Final Product

The final product will be marked based on accurate and complete reproduction of the pattern in measurements and design. The planes need to be smooth and flat. The angles need to be sharp. Finally, the symmetry and orientation of the two ends and the middle play an important part of the grading. There are some applicants who will get the ends in the wrong place, or invert a triangular end, or have the saddle on the wrong side and etc. If there are incomplete ends you will lose marks on not having a complete and accurate reproduction of the pattern and lack of symmetry and orientation of the three parts. So, it is very important that you attempt all surfaces rather than trying to perfect one or two. Even if you have very good carvings on a few parts of the soap, you will not score competitively if you don't complete the carving by at least attempting to carve all surfaces.

Warnings

Some warnings and tips are to check all dimensions regularly by referring back to the top, side, bottom, and end views. You don't want to carve over the lines you marked because there is no room for correction for over carving. So, beware of where the lines that define the edges are and be careful not to carve over them. Many applicants will find that the time constraint for carving to be a major problem. Some will try to save time by cutting away chunks, but this will lead to chipping and crumbling of the soap irreparably. It also results in the risk of carving too much such that there is no chance of rectifying the dimension or shape. The key is to manage time well and remove a little of the soap at a time but at a faster pace. You will need to manage time between marking the soap, coarse carving and fine carving. Following the recommended time allocation for carving is very important for proper time management in the carving section.

Exam Day

Carving materials for the carving section will be provided including the handle, blade, ruler, soap, Sharpie marker, and pencil. So, you do not need to bring the basic carving materials such as your own blade, handle, ruler, marker and soap. However, you should take extra pencils that are pre-sharpened and a pencil sharpener. In addition, you should also bring a pair of latex gloves to keep the soap dry from perspiration and a few bandages in case of accidental cutting.

Practice Problems

All measurements are in millimeters (not necessarily drawn to scale).

Directions for Carving:

The illustrations near the top show how the carving should appear when it is completed.

The carving exercise consists of 3 parts (2 end and 1 surface pattern). It is important that all 3 parts be completed to be considered for high scoring.

You may use the small ridge on the top and bottom as midlines for carving relationships.

The dimensions should be followed as closely as possible. The carving will be evaluated on accurate and complete reproduction of the pattern in measurements and design, smoothness and flatness of planes, sharpness of angles, symmetry and orientation of the 3 parts.

DIRECTIONS FOR HANDING IN THE CARVING:

1. Print your name, identification number and test centre code on an uncut surface of your carving and also on the napkin.

2. Wrap your carving carefully and securely so that it may be shipped safely for grading. Fold the napkin in such a way that the carving will not fall out.

3. Hand in your wrapped carving to your evaluation proctor.

   ▧ Shaded area denotes cut surface.

   *This dimension can vary depending on the overall length of the carving.

Carving Design #1

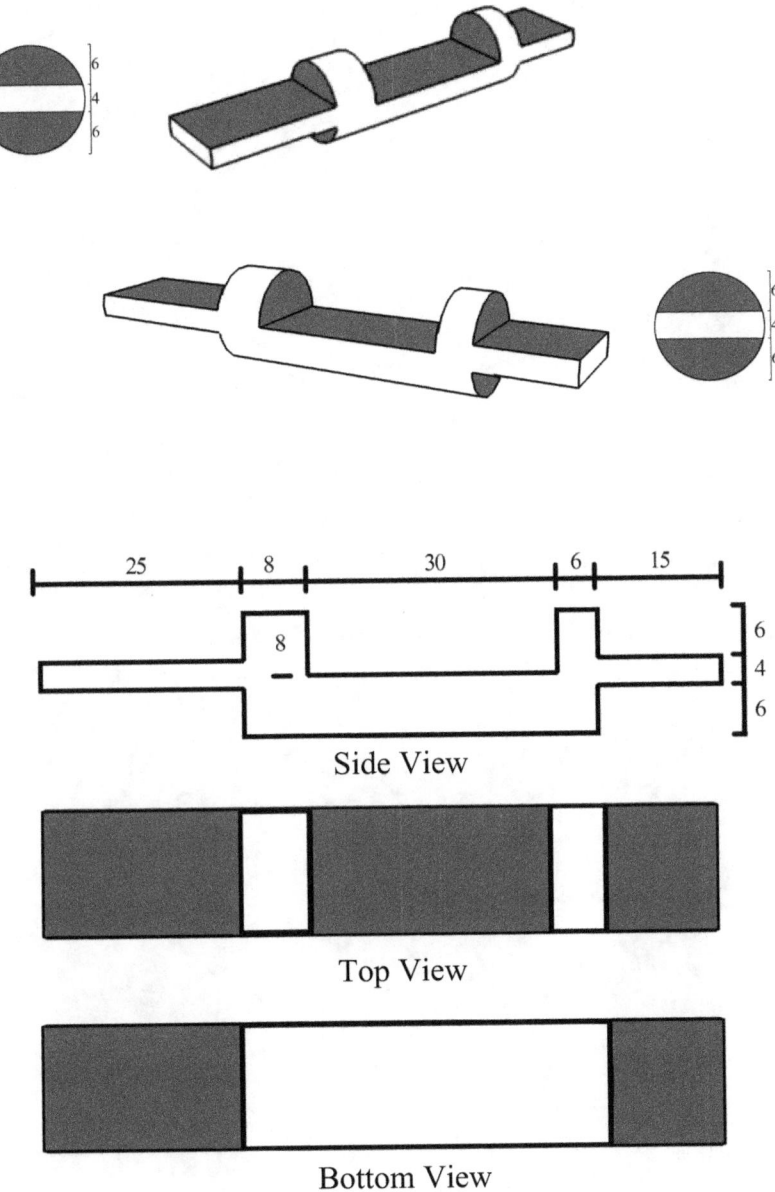

Side View

Top View

Bottom View

Carving Design #2

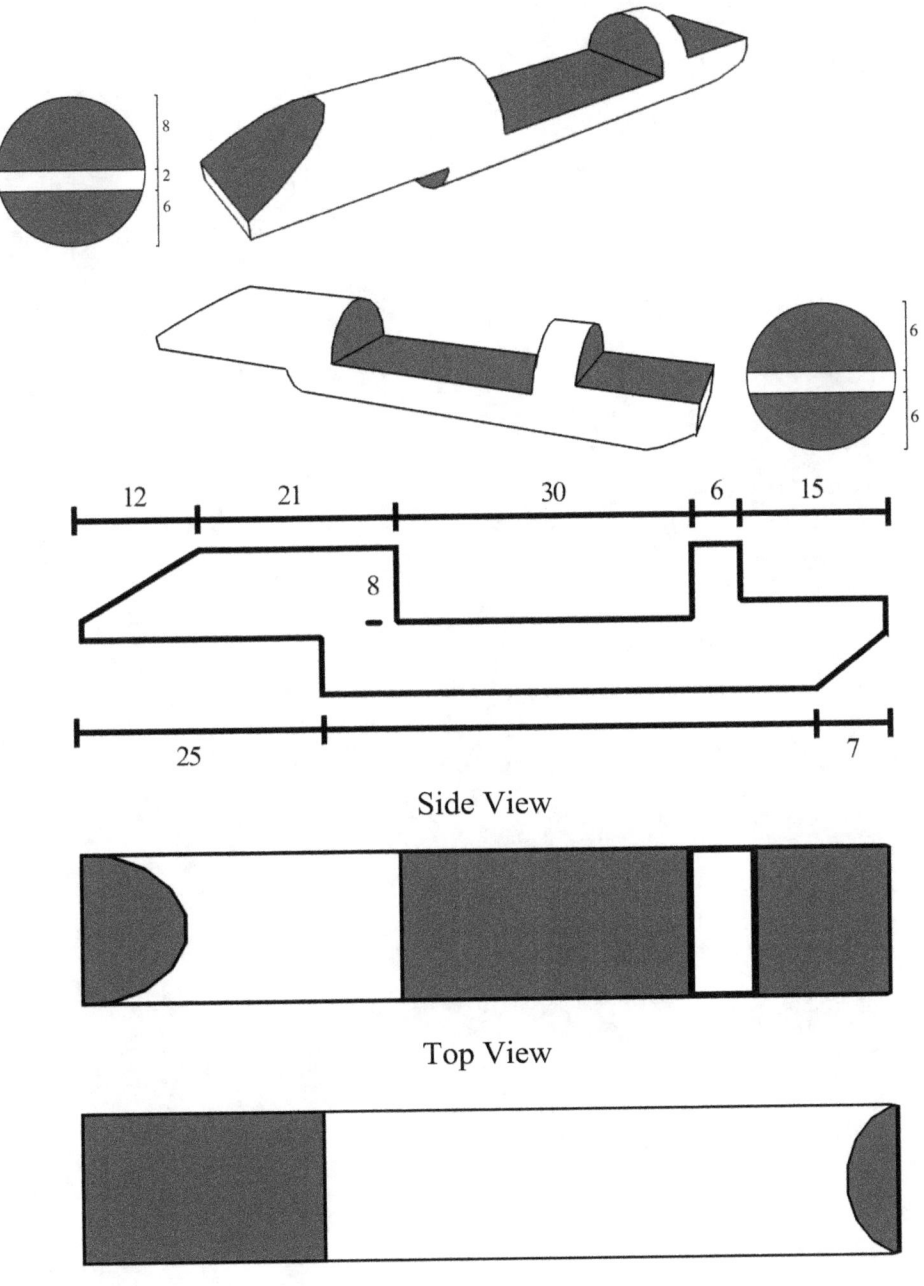

Side View

Top View

Bottom View

Carving Design #3

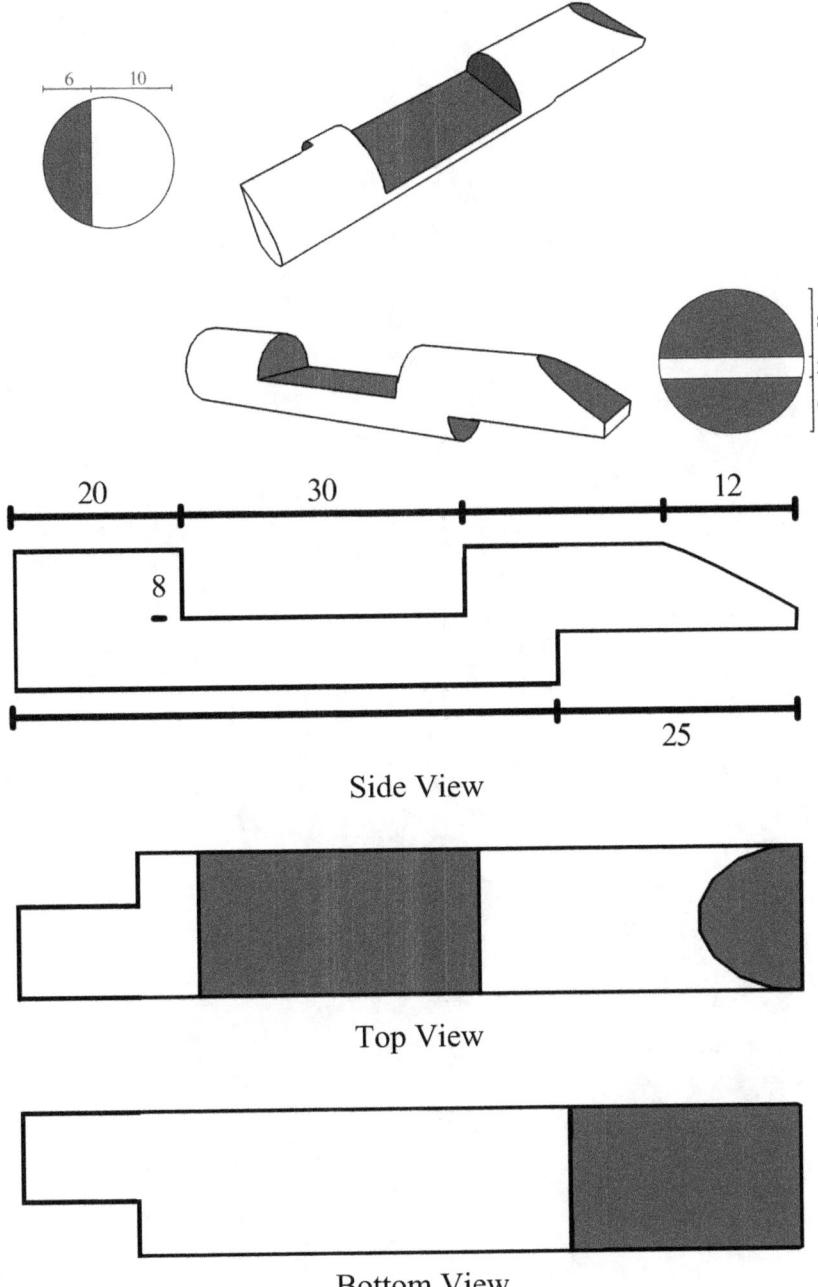

Side View

Top View

Bottom View

Carving Design #4

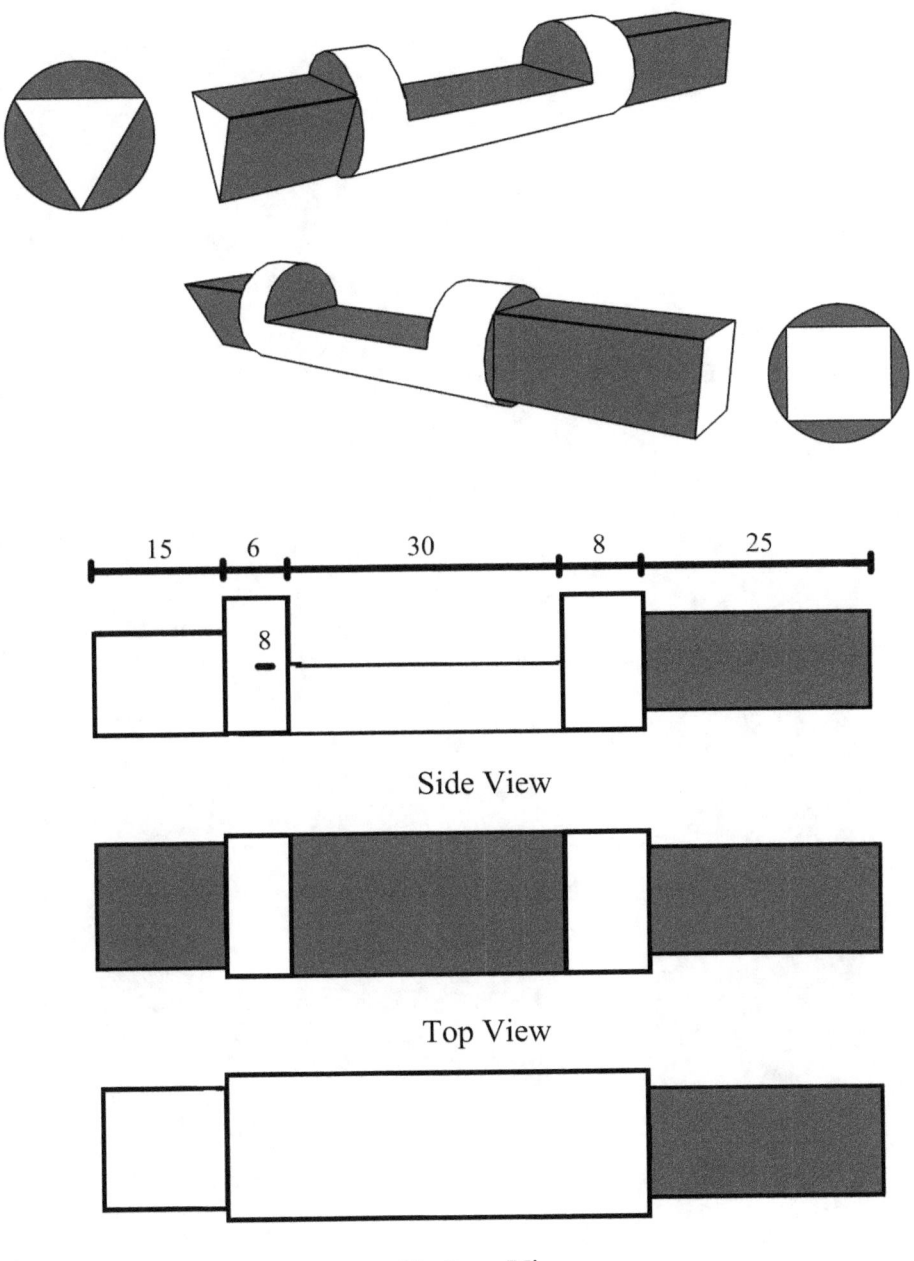

Side View

Top View

Bottom View

Carving Design #5

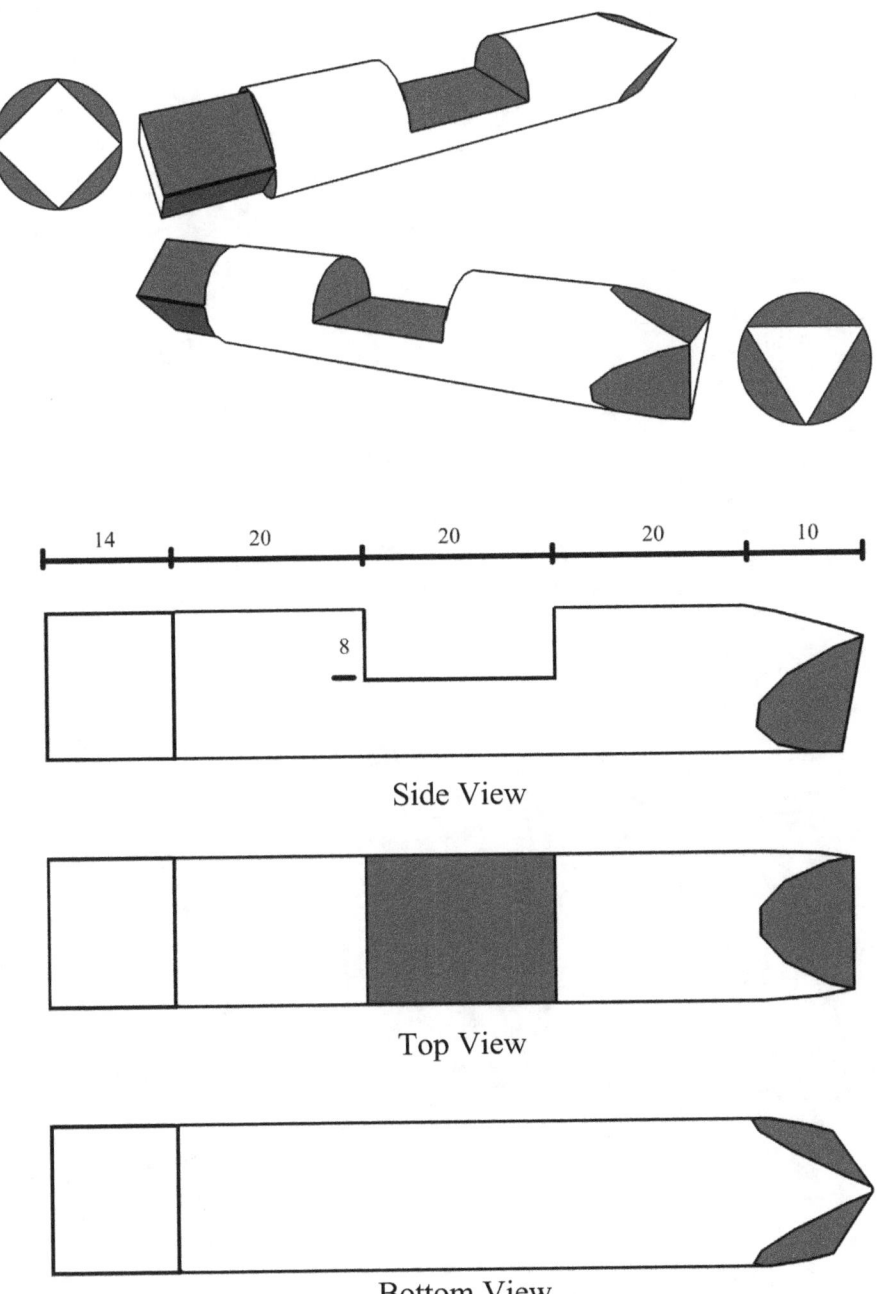

Side View

Top View

Bottom View

Carving Design #6

Side View

Top View

Bottom View

MORE PRACTICE PROBLEMS AVAILABLE WITH THE

Canadian Dental Aptitude Test (DAT)

Soap Carving Practice Problem Series

www.ingramcontent.com/pod-product-compliance
Lightning Source LLC
Chambersburg PA
CBHW071415300426
44114CB00016B/2307